fabric types

HAZEL KING

Heinemann
LIBRARY

www.heinemann.co.uk
Visit our website to find out more information about Heinemann Library books.

To order:
Phone 44 (0) 1865 888066
Send a fax to 44 (0) 1865 314091
Visit the Heinemann Bookshop at www.heinemann.co.uk to browse our catalogue and order online.

First published in Great Britain by Heinemann Library,
Halley Court, Jordan Hill, Oxford OX2 8EJ,
a division of Reed Educational and Professional Publishing Ltd.
Heinemann is a registered trademark of Reed Educational & Professional Publishing Limited.

OXFORD MELBOURNE AUCKLAND
JOHANNESBURG BLANTYRE GABORONE
IBADAN PORTSMOUTH NH (USA) CHICAGO

Designed by AMR
Illustrations by Art Construction
Originated by Ambassador Litho Ltd
Printed in Hong Kong/China

ISBN 0 431 10561 8 (hardback)
04 03 02 01 00
10 9 8 7 6 5 4 3 2 1

ISBN 0 431 10579 0 (paperback)
05 04 03 02 01
10 9 8 7 6 5 4 3 2 1

British Library Cataloguing in Publication Data
King, Hazel
Fabric types. – (Trends in textile technology)
1.Textile fabrics – Juvenile literature
I.Title
677

Acknowledgements
The Publishers would like to thank the following for permission to reproduce photographs:
Eye Ubiquitous/Helen Lisher, p.23 ; Gareth Boden, pp.5, 15, 27, 33, 43; Hunters of Brora, p.21; Image Bank/John Kelly, p.26; Marks & Spencer Plc, p.20; Meg Sullivan, p.8; Performing Arts Library/Lara Platman, p.11; Robert Harding/GE Magazines, p.38; Sarah Lawrence, p.19; ScotWeave, p.9; Tony Stone/Chris Windsor, p.34; Trip: J Ringland p. 41, A Tovy, p.13.

Cover photograph reproduced with permission of Corbis.

Our thanks to Andy Rumsby for his comments in the preparation of this book.

Any words appearing in the text in bold, **like this**, are explained in the glossary.

contents

what is weaving?	4
weaving patterns	6
industrial weaving	8
knitting patterns	10
industrial knitting	12
bonded fabrics	14
making felt	16
using felt – a case study	18
manufacturing fabrics	20
open-work fabrics	22
creative carpets	24
functional fabrics	26
working clothes – a case study	28
protective fabrics	30
fashionable fleece	32
stretch fabrics	34
textile projects	36
recycling fabrics	38
versatile textile	40
fabric technology	42
resources	44
glossary	46
index	48

what is weaving?

The creation of textiles is one of the oldest and perhaps most important crafts of civilized communities. Britain is regarded as the birthplace of textile manufacture, but since its hey-day in the mid-nineteenth century, weaving has spread to become a worldwide industry. Evidence of weaving techniques come from a range of countries, dating as far back as 5000 BCE.

Textile evidence

Very often, evidence of activities in the past is found in inscriptions, carvings or pictures rather than actual examples. From an inscription describing the work of weavers, it is known that weaving was carried out in Mesopotamia in Iraq as early as 4200 BCE. Pictures and writing show that weaving and other textile activities were carried out by the Sumerians in 3000 BCE. In hot climates, linen and cotton were the favoured **yarns**. Linen was made in Egypt, for example, and cotton was spun in India. People in colder climates such as northern Europe preferred to use wool. In Britain during Roman times a state weaving mill was established to supply uniforms to the Roman army.

Women's work

In Britain, as well as many other countries, the crafts of spinning and weaving were traditionally carried out by women, usually in the home. After weaving the fabrics they would sew them to make clothing for the family or other necessary fabric items for the house. It was a fairly sedate occupation which required patience rather than strength, and even today many 'homeworkers' are women who contribute to the production of textile items. As demand for textile items increased and as technology developed, so weaving became more mechanized. Large, heavy looms replaced the handheld variety, and men became involved in the business of textiles.

Weaving today

Weaving has advanced considerably over the last 200 years, mainly owing to technological developments, and today it remains an important industry in Britain. Weaving may be defined as the interlacing of yarns at right angles to one another. In order to understand the technique of weaving it is important to first clarify some of the terms used.

Firstly, fibres are the basis of all woven fabrics. Fibres are spun together to form yarns, and yarns are woven into fabrics.

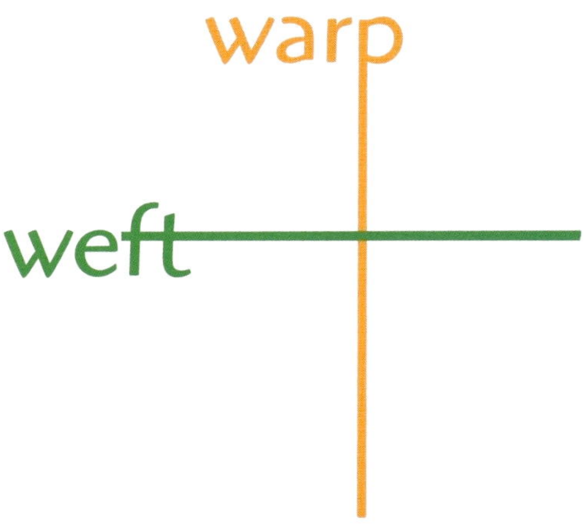

▲ *Two sets of yarns are used when weaving; **warp** yarns run the length of the fabric, and **weft** yarns run the width of the fabric.*

The warp yarns are called **ends** and the weft yarns are called **picks**. So, weaving involves a series of picks passing under or over a series of ends to form a specified pattern. Obviously the picks have to turn each time they reach the edge of the fabric in order to form the next row. This edge is called the selvedge, and its function is to stop the outside ends fraying from the body of the fabric. In order to make the selvedge more secure, stronger warp yarns are used at the edges. A selvedge is formed when the pick turns at the last end. This is known as a hairpin selvedge. However, today some (shuttleless) looms do not weave fabrics with selvedges, but leave ends sticking out at the fabric edges.

Against the grain

Because woven fabric is produced when yarns are interlaced at right angles to one another, it must consist of two sets of yarns. One set has parallel yarns running down the length of the fabric, and the other set has parallel yarns running across the width. The parallel yarns provide the fabric with its grain. A fabric's grain means the direction in which the yarns travel, so all woven fabrics have two grains.

Feeling bias

Imagine holding a piece of woven fabric along its weft grain and pulling hard. How much does it stretch? Usually fabrics that have been woven don't stretch very much along their grain. However, there is more 'give' or stretch in woven fabrics across their **bias**. If a square of woven fabric is folded in half to form a triangle, the longest edge of the triangle is the fabric's bias. In other words it is where the grains cross diagonally, and it is at this point that the fabric has maximum stretch. Often during textile production certain parts may have to be cut out 'on the bias' so that they form the appropriate shape. Components of a soft toy may need to be cut out on the bias or perhaps the collar of a shirt so that it can bend sufficiently when being sewn on to the opening of a neck.

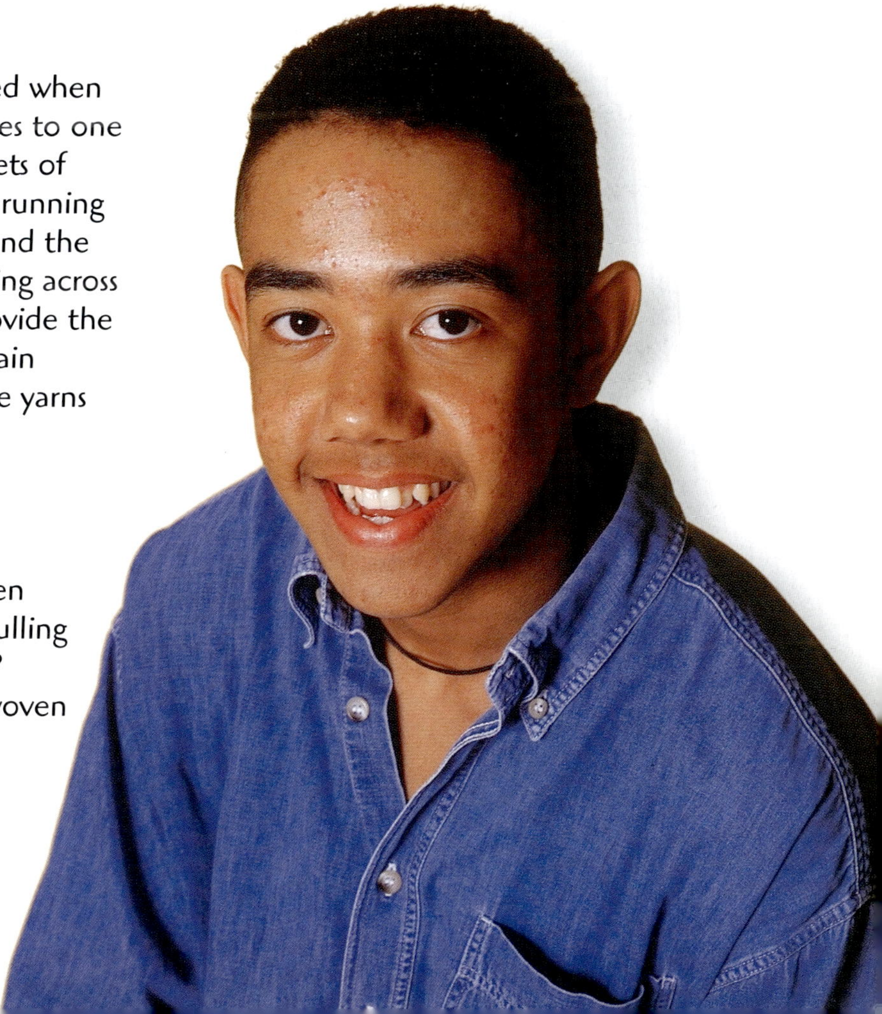

The fabric of a collar may be cut on the bias to allow it to curve around the neck.

weaving patterns

Weaving is carried out using a loom. The loom can be very, very simple, as in the diagram below, or it can be an industrial loom, such as the air jet, which can produce over 1500 metres of fabric per minute.

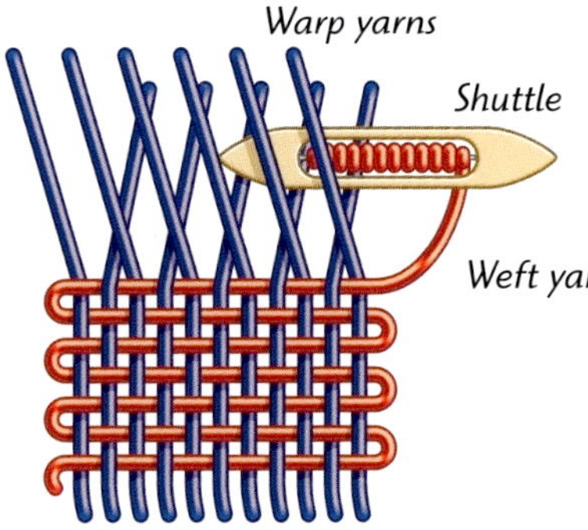

▲ *In a simple loom, the shuttle carries the weft yarn over and under the warp yarns.*

Principle of weaving

The basic principle of weaving is the same for all types of loom; the loom is set with **warp yarns** (ends) and the shuttle is threaded with **weft** yarns (picks). The shuttle carries the weft yarn over and under the warp yarns to form the first row of fabric. As the process continues so the fabric develops. The picks must be pushed towards the previous weft yarn to ensure the fabric is strong and evenly woven.

Frames and beams

In order for the shuttle to move swiftly over and under the ends, groups of warp threads are lifted up and down by a frame known as a **heddle**. The loom is set up for the particular weave that it is to create, and the warp threads are lifted and lowered, according to the desired pattern, by the heddle shafts. As you can see in the diagram below, the reed holds the lifted warp ends as the shuttle passes through with the weft yarn. As the fabric develops it winds round the cloth beam at the end of the process.

Different patterns

Different patterns can be created in woven fabrics by altering the order in which the weft yarn travels over or under the warp yarns. Three main weaves are plain, twill and sateen.

Plain weave

Plain weave is the simplest as it involves a series of 'over and under' moves by the weft yarn. The pattern begins with the weft yarn passing over one warp yarn,

▼ *This basic loom shows how fabric can be created through weaving.*

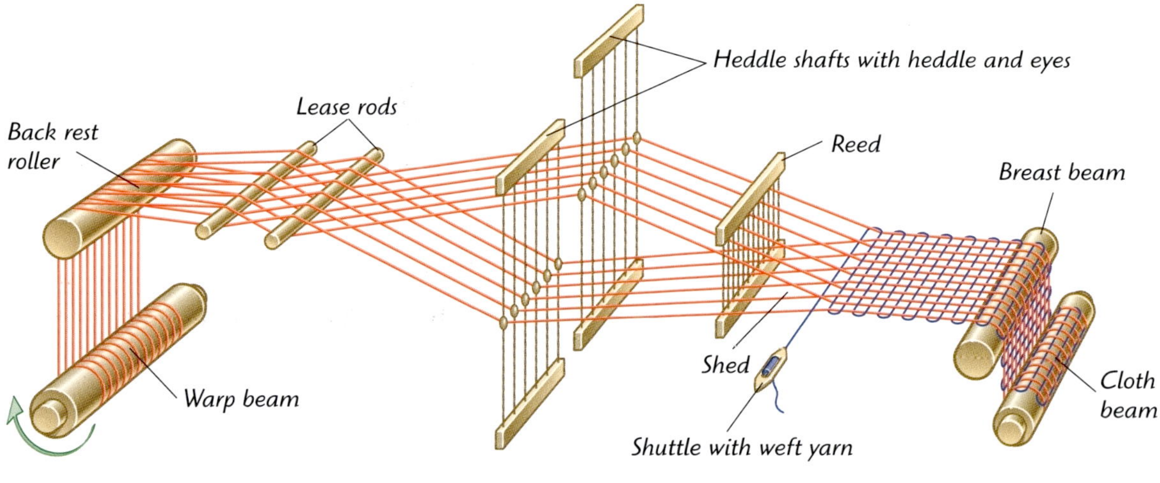

then under the next. This continues until the end of the row. The opposite process occurs in the second row. These two rows form the plain pattern, which is repeated throughout.

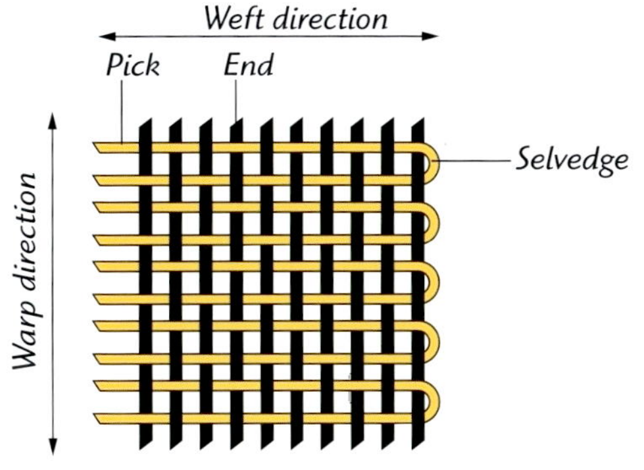

Plain weave fabric is very popular although the weave itself is quite featureless.

End-uses for this type of fabric include surgical dressings for bandages, parachute fabric, fabric for shoes or tents, and sheeting fabric.

Twill weave

Twill weave has a diagonal pattern created by the weft yarns passing over two and under two warp yarns in the first row, then the order moving one thread along in the next row. The number of yarns involved can vary, but if the

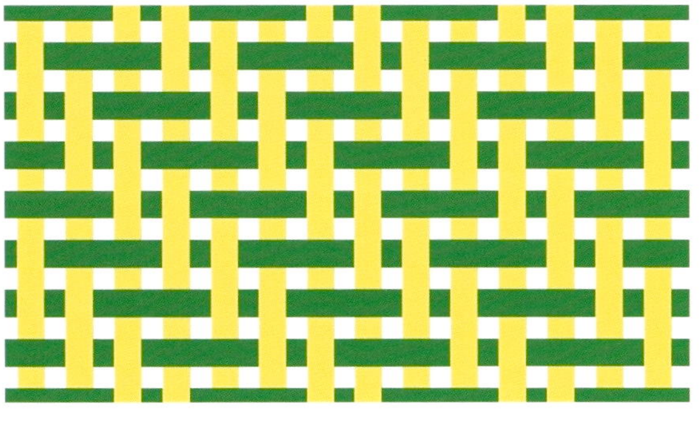

A twill weave fabric may be used for jeans, suits and trousers.

number of warp and weft yarns are equal, the pattern is said to be a balanced twill.

If the diagonal design runs from the bottom left of the fabric up to the top right, the twill is known as a Z twill. If it runs in the opposite direction it is called an S twill. 'Herringbone' is an example of a twill weave, and fabric made to this design is often used in suits and trousers.

Sateen weave

Sateen weave is clearly recognized by its shiny right side. The design is created by passing weft yarns over several warp yarns (between four and eight), then under one. The point at which the weft goes under the warp must not be next to that point in the row above or below.

A sateen weave produces a smooth, lustrous surface. Satin is an example.

Weaving a design

Textile designers can show a weaving process by representing the design on squared paper. Coloured pens are used to represent the actual pattern. They must also indicate the type of yarns to use. Today, designs for woven fabric can be produced very quickly using computer software.

industrial weaving

Weaving is carried out on what is commonly called a loom, although today it is sometimes referred to as a weaving machine. This term reflects the high standard of precision engineering used in the manufacture of modern looms.

Weft insertion

From the basic principle of weaving we can see that the **weft** must pass between the **warp yarns**, a process usually referred to as weft insertion. The traditional way to do this is via a shuttle, but modern machines use methods such as projectile, rapier, air jet and water jet, as explained below.

A Jacquard loom. A series of cards control the lifting and lowering of the warp yarns. These cards can be seen at the top of the photograph.

Projectile

A Swiss machine manufacturer, Sulzer, introduced a loom in the 1950s which used a number of 'projectiles'. The projectiles are like shuttles, but instead of the weft being wound around them, they 'grab' the weft from the left-hand edge of the fabric and pull it across to form a row. The projectile then releases the weft yarn and returns to the left-hand edge while another projectile shoots across. On one of the most popular loom widths, 3300 millimetres, up to seventeen projectiles are used in sequence. This system produces fabric very fast.

Rapier systems

There are a variety of rapier systems used in weaving production, but generally they do not work at the high speeds achieved by projectile weft insertion. Rapier systems can produce fabric at around 800 metres per minute, compared with 1100 metres per minute for projectile systems. However, rapier weft insertion is popular for fancy weaving, especially when there are frequent changes of pattern.

Air and water jet

The principle of these looms is that the weft yarn is carried across the warp ends by powerful jets of either air or water. Air jets have the advantage of speed and can produce fabric at rates of over 1500 metres per minute. Water jets have the obvious disadvantage of being suitable only for yarns that do not absorb water. However, they are still used to weave **polyamide** fabrics, which are used for such items as tarpaulins, anoraks, parachutes and overalls. They can achieve speeds of over 1400 metres per minute.

Jacquard and dobby looms

Jacquard looms weave complicated patterns, and produce high-quality, expensive fabrics. The traditional Jacquard looms work by using a series of cards to control the lifting and lowering of the warp yarns. These cards contain the weave design in the sequence (order) in which it should appear on the fabric. This system allows complicated designs to be produced because single yarns can be raised according to the preset pattern. However, today computers are widely used for designing patterns for weaving, and details of the design are stored on disk. The disk is then used to feed an electronic memory unit connected to the Jacquard. Once the pattern has been stored in the memory the disk can be removed and used on another weaving machine.

Dobby looms are used to weave fairly simple patterns, and a series of shafts and pegs, rather than cards, control the warp yarns.

Computerized weaving

What started as a research project at the Scottish College of Textiles, Galashiels, has ended up as a highly successful commercial venture in the world of weaving. The project was to develop a computer-aided design (CAD) package that could create designs for use with Jacquard and dobby looms.

Traditional methods of producing designs for weaving were very time-consuming. Although the looms themselves had become highly technical, the design process prior to weaving had not; that is until the new computerized system known as ScotWeave.

The ScotWeave package enables all manner of designs to be created in any fabric. The design and measurements can be seen both on-screen and as a printout, so the designers can actually see the effect of the weave before it is manufactured. It is perhaps not surprising that this **innovation** came out of Scotland, because traditionally Scottish fabrics have intricate patterns with lots of **colourways**. The CAD package can show sixteen million colours on-screen!

ScotWeave was first sold to textile industries in 1984. Today over 250 ScotWeave systems are in use worldwide. In 1999 ScotWeave Ltd, the company which develops and markets the design system, launched a Microsoft Windows-compatible version of ScotWeave.

The ScotWeave computer-aided design program enables all manner of designs to be created in any fabric, quickly and economically.

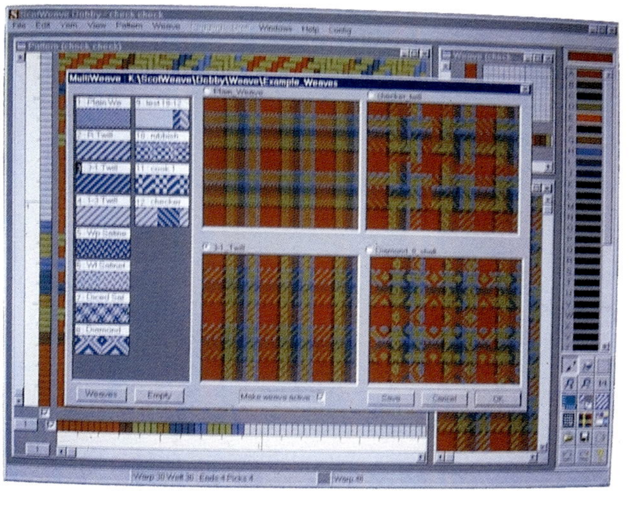

knitting patterns

Knitting is the second main method of fabric production after weaving. It involves the interlocking of loops of **yarn** to form a fabric. The traditional way to do this is by hand, using two knitting needles, and it is thought to have been practised as early as the fifth century. However, in 1589 the Reverend William Lee invented the 'stocking frame', which began the development of machine knitting technology.

Today the knitting industry is divided into two distinct areas, **weft** knitting and **warp** knitting.

Weft knitting

Weft knitting is the simplest method of converting a yarn into a fabric. It is also the most versatile, because it can use a variety of different yarn types and produces a wide range of fabric structures. In weft knitting, loops are formed across the width of the fabric and interlocked with loops above and below them. Only one yarn, or cone of yarn, is necessary, although demand for more production means circular weft knitting machines are being used with up to 192 threads. All hand knitting is weft knitting.

Courses and wales

The diagram on this page illustrates simple, plain knitted structures. The term 'course' refers to the rows of loops across the width of the fabric. It is used as a measurement because the number of courses determines the length of the fabric. The wale, on the other hand, refers to the column of needle loops, so it determines the fabrics width.

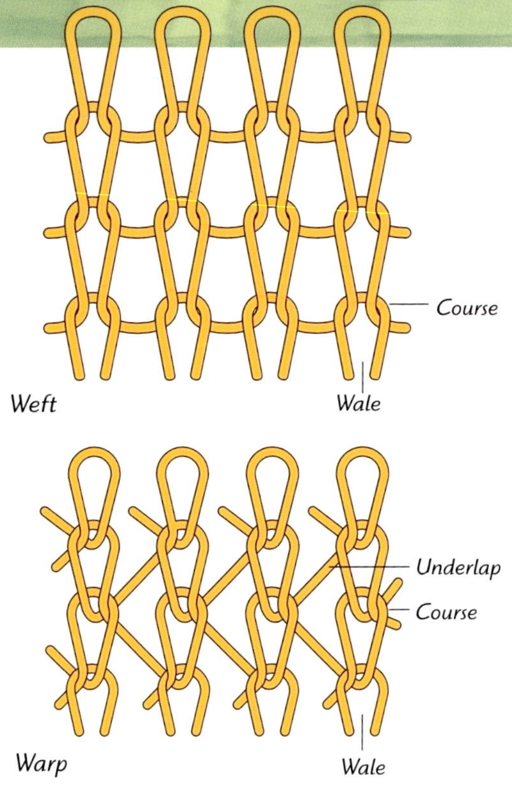

Weft and warp knitting. A row of loops is known as a course while a column of loops is called a wale.

There are basically four types of weft knitted fabrics: plain single jersey, rib, purl and interlock.

Plain single jersey is the simplest that is possible with one set of needles. It is widely used in the manufacture of knitted outer wear, footwear and all types of clothing.

Rib or double jersey fabrics have the ability to stretch width-ways and so are used for cuffs, waistbands, collars and 'stretch to fit' garments.

The structure of purl fabrics means there is plenty of scope for patterns, which makes them ideal for children's clothing.

Interlock knitted fabrics are reversible with a smooth surface on both sides. Fine yarns are often used for interlocking because the fabrics tend to be thicker and heavier. They are used in the manufacture of skirts, dresses and underwear.

Warp knitting

Warp knitting is the fastest method of fabric production using mainly **continuous filament** yarns. A wide variety of yarn types may be used. A fabric is created by interlocking loops of yarn down the length of the fabric. This type of knitting cannot be produced by hand. The diagram shows a simple warp knitting structure.

Knitted movement

Knitted fabrics have a clear advantage over woven types as they allow more movement. This can be illustrated by the choice of fabrics for garments that require a huge flexibility – for example, dancers' costumes.

Knitting at home

Domestic knitting machines can be placed on a table or work surface and are relatively easy to operate, either by hand or electronically. They knit much faster than a person can knit by hand, and consist of a series of needles set in 'beds' with a carriage which passes over them. Some varieties produce patterns automatically through a punch card system or by scanning a pattern to electronic circuits. Computer graphics packages allow you to design and produce unique textile items.

However, hand knitting is trendy again – even supermodels have been caught clicking needles between shows in an effort to create the ultimate in knitwear.

The knitted Shantung® fabric has the ability to float and move with the body. It is an easy-care fabric and is ideal for dancers who need to move freely and in comfort.

industrial knitting

Industrial knitting machines produce fabric in flat knitted form or in circular tubes. There are three main needle types used in machine knitting. Latch needles are 'self-acting'; compound needles consist of two parts; and bearded needles (which are similar to latch needles but have only one part) have to be controlled by some other means. All knitting machines use one or more of these three types, although the latch needle is probably the most popular in **weft** knitting. The illustration shows very simply how a latch needle works.

The action of a latch needle in industrial knitting.

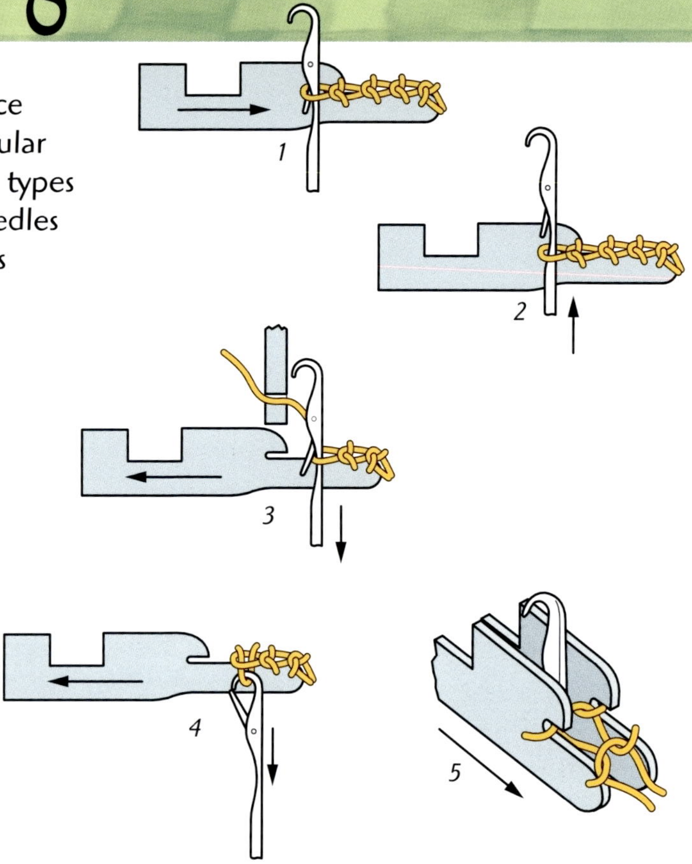

Weft knitting machines

Weft knitting machines range from high-output but limited-capacity types, to versatile multi-**functional** types with the ability to produce elaborate patterns. The machines themselves can be classified according to the variety of needle used and whether they produce flat or circular fabrics.

Machines use different numbers of needles, usually one or two sets of needle 'beds', which may be arranged in a straight line (as in the flat-bar and straight-bar machines) or around a cylinder (as in the circular machines).

Warp knitting machines

Two types of machine are used for the production of **warp** knitted fabrics: Tricot and Raschel. Tricot machines are the simplest and can use both bearded and compound needles. They tend to use **continuous filament yarns** and are used in the production of fabrics for clothes and household items. Raschel machines use latch and compound needles, and usually have a greater number of needles than the Tricot machines. They are used industrially for the production of furnishings and Jacquard fabrics (see page 9).

One set of yarns can be used in warp machine knitting, but usually two sets are used to produce fabrics for lingerie or thicker fabrics for garments and bedclothes. Raised-loop fabrics can also be made, while plain and fancy net and mesh fabrics are produced for curtains.

Joining up

Weft knitted fabrics tend to curl at the edges and ladder if they are cut, so they cannot easily be cut and joined when making textile items. With hand knitting this is not a problem, because the item or garment is knitted in shaped pieces which are then sewn together. Circular knitting machines can be used to produce fabrics for items without seams, as long as the correct width of machine is available.

Warp knitted fabrics can be cut and sewn just like woven fabrics.

The way knitted garments are assembled is very important, because the technique must produce seams with similar properties to the knitting itself. The joining techniques usually employed include overlocking, seaming, and linking, which are types of stitching that produce flat seams.

Diving ahead

Surprising though it may seem, knitted fabrics are at the forefront of technological developments in textiles! Raschel machines have recently been used in the production of fabrics for a very specific market – diving suits. The fabrics are known as knitted 'spacer' structures, as they consist of layers of fabric with areas of space between the two surfaces. The fibre CoolMax™ is used for the surface next to the diver's skin, and the hollow channel provides extra air-conditioning to improve comfort.

Innovative bras

Another recent **innovation** in the world of industrial knitting comes from an Italian company who are designing bras. The idea is for bras to be manufactured on circular knitting machines where the underwires can be incorporated directly into hollow spaces formed by the tubular knitting process. By means of a particular way of controlling the needles, it is possible to knit tubes with bend, which is clearly an important requirement of a bra.

Knitted 'spacer' structures are used in the manufacture of fabric for diving suits.

bonded fabrics

Bonded fabrics are part of the group of non-woven fabrics made directly from fibres, without first being made into **yarns**. These fabrics do not have an organized structure like woven and knitted fabrics, and therefore possess very different properties.

Bonded properties

The properties of bonded fabrics are wide-ranging and may include anything from 'soft to the touch' to 'very rough' or 'impossible to tear' to 'extremely weak'. Clearly this means a huge variety of items can be manufactured using bonded fabrics – disposable nappies, teabags, operating theatre gowns, dish cloths, underfelt for carpets, and fabrics used in civil engineering (known as **geotextiles**).

One of the main advantages of bonded fabrics is that they can be produced more cheaply and easily than woven and knitted fabrics. This is because they require fewer preparation processes during their manufacture. This makes them particularly well suited to the production of disposable items.

Making bonded fabrics

The first step in the production of bonded fabrics is to make a 'web' which forms the basis of the fabric. Webs are made using a variety of different methods, and both **staple fibres** and **continuous filaments** are used. The fibres within the web may be arranged in one direction, in more than one direction or completely at random.

The second step is then to bond the fibres within the web using one of a number of methods:

- adhesive bonding
- thermal bonding
- needle punching
- stitch bonding
- hydroentangling.

Sometimes a combination of methods is used.

Adhesive bonding

The technique of adhesive bonding involves applying an adhesive to the web fibres. Several different adhesives may be used for this, but the choice is based on the type of fibres and the fabric's end-use.

The main methods of applying adhesive

Saturation
simplest method; web is saturated in a bath of adhesive, then passed between rollers; suitable for stiff, compact fabrics

Spray
sprayers arranged over a moving web; adhesive sprayed on to surface layer

Foam-impregnation
web passes through a foam box where foam, air and adhesive are applied; then dried in a drying unit; suitable for lightweight webs

Print
adhesive is printed on to the web at certain points, then heated; suitable for production of fabric for disposable cloths

Just some of the everyday end-uses for bonded fabrics.

Thermal bonding

Thermal bonded fabrics are produced by the application of heat, often together with other bonding techniques such as needle punching. Webs of fibres with low melting points are fused by the action of heat as they pass between heated rollers. These fabrics can have rather unusual uses – such as in the fuel tanks of military helicopters, where they function as explosion-suppression structures!

Needle punching

This method of bonding uses needles to force web fibres into a tuft on the surface of the fabric. The needles are special triangular 'barbed' needles, which have three jagged edges on each of the three corners. The needle punching machine contains several thousand of these barbed needles, which punch the web-forcing fibres through to the other side, where they remain as the needle is withdrawn. Needle punched fabrics are used for blankets, shoe lining materials, paper-maker's felt, medical fabrics, air filters and floor coverings.

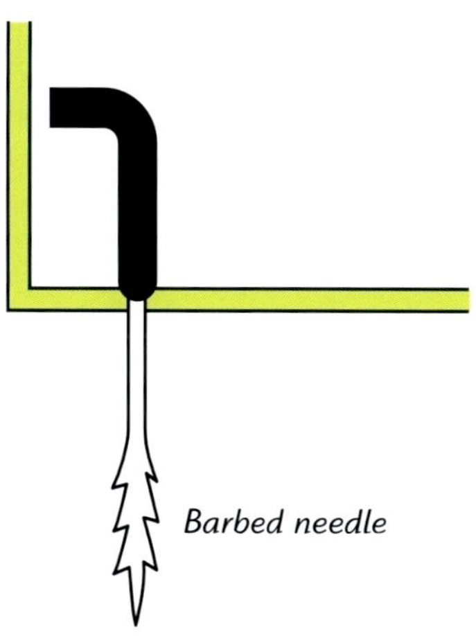

A barbed needle has three jagged edges and is used to produce tufts of fibres on the surface of needle punched fabric.

Hydroentangled

As the name suggests, with this bonding method the fabrics are formed as pressurized jets of water cause the fibres to become entangled. There is usually an adhesive bonding stage as well. These fabrics are often made of polyester fibres and are used for home furnishings and industrial fabrics.

Stitch bonding

The machine used to carry out stitch bonding is basically a modified **warp** knitting machine that bonds the fibres by knitting columns of stitches down the length of the web. Sometimes the web goes through a **tacking** process first, to ensure there is a good interlocking of fibres when it is stitch bonded. Fabrics produced by this method may be used for specialized purposes – for example, in medical products such as dressings and bandages, or as covers for moulded components such as the headrests in a car.

making felt

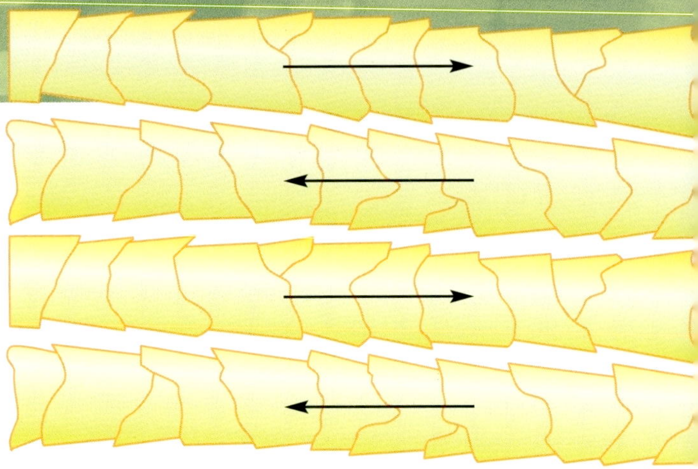

▲ *The rachet effect of felting, caused by wool's scaly surface.*

Felt is a dense fabric with a matted appearance. It is one of the oldest non-woven fabrics, and is generally made using 100% wool, although other hair fibres and wool blends are sometimes included. A simple explanation of the production of felt would be the entangling of fibres through the application of moisture, heat and agitation (vigorous movement).

Felting

You can apply the term 'felting' to the making of felt, as well as to the rather less desirable outcome of hair fibres felting or matting if they are washed at too high a temperature, or too vigorously. Felting is something all hair fibres, especially wool, will do if subjected to enough moisture, heat and agitation. This is because of their scaly surface as well as their elasticity and high crimp (waviness).

Rachet effect

The diagram represents two magnified wool fibres and their scaly surface. The scales have roots and tips, and these always lie in the same direction – so any movement between fibres is possible in one direction only. The arrows in the diagram indicate that if fibres are forced in opposite directions there is a rachet effect and the fibre tips catch, causing them to tangle.

If felting occurs accidentally (perhaps during the washing process) the item shrinks because the fibres have been moved closer together.

Properties of felt

The felting process uses a very different method of binding fibres from those used for woven or knitted fabrics, but felt can be just as strong. Obviously it cannot be washed in the conventional way and has to be sponged clean with warm soapy water. One big advantage of felt is that it does not fray or unravel. End-uses for felt fabrics include hats, slippers, fancy dress costumes and non-scratch backing for ornaments and trophies.

Milling

Milling is the term used to describe the process of felting wool, and traditionally this has been carried out in a rotary milling machine. The machine consists of a bath of liquid at the bottom, rollers, and a stuffer box. The liquid usually contains a soap which acts as a **lubricant** to encourage movement between the fibres. The fabric passes between the rollers and is then forced into the stuffer box, causing the fabric to fold up randomly. Sometimes pressure is applied to the top of the stuffer box, which increases the pressure on the fabric to bend. The fabric passes continually through these three areas in a circular movement, until the desired end-result is achieved. Both the heat and moisture make the fibres swollen and flexible.

Modern methods

Today's milling machines are based on the traditional ones, but the stuffer box is generally more complex. They also have controls for stopping the process when a preset length has been formed.

In order to achieve a high-quality end-product, further controls can be placed on the fabric speed, the temperature and **pH** of the liquid, and the pressure of the rollers and stuffer box.

Make your own felt

Felt can be made very easily by hand. This felt-making method has been supplied by Sarah Lawrence (see page 18). Pre-dyed fleece produces a colourful end-result. Unless you want to create a random pattern of colour, make sure you have an idea for a design before you start.

Resources

- bubble wrap
- net (e.g. a piece of old net curtain)
- shallow tray (e.g. cat litter tray)
- jar and screw-top lid containing a few small holes
- Merino 70 wool fleece, pre-dyed
- Lux soap flakes

1 Cut bubble wrap and net to fit inside shallow tray. Lay bubble wrap, bubble-side up, in tray. Half fill jar with warm water.

2 Decide which colour fleece to have as bottom layer; gently tease out some fibres. Lay them all in same direction on bubble wrap; leave a border of 5cm along each edge. Continue until bottom layer is about 1cm thick.

3 Choose a different colour fleece for next layer and tease out fibres as before. This time, lay fibres so they lie in the opposite direction to first layer. Make sure this layer is also about 1cm thick. This forms the base of the felt.

4 Still continuing 'cross-over' layering, add patches of coloured fleece to felt base to create a pattern or design. This should be about 1cm thick.

5 Carefully place net on top of felt to keep fibres in place; sprinkle with a few flakes of Lux soap. Sprinkle warm water over net using jar. Do not soak felt; fibres need to be wetted not floating in water!

6 **Pre-felting** process: carefully lift net, rub felt gently with hands (use a little soap if needed). Continue rubbing until fibres start moving towards the back of the felt.

7 **Hardening**: fold edges of bubble wrap inwards, then roll felt into tight sausage, squeezing out excess water. Roll sausage like a rolling-pin for a few minutes; unroll; re-roll in opposite direction. Roll for another few minutes. Repeat three times.

8 Unroll and check to see whether enough felting has taken place (try to pinch some fibres between your fingers, the fibres should stay intact). Leave piece of felt to dry. (This felt is suitable for both hand and machine embroidery.)

9 Milling: Further rolling makes the felt dense and firm. The felt is now suitable for garments.

using felt – a case study

The craft of felt-making developed long ago, in many parts of the world. Felt is one of the oldest textiles known, being used before fibres were spun or fabric was woven. It has been made for thousands of years in Central Asia by **nomadic** tribes using wool and hair from their sheep, goats, camels and horses.

In the Western world it was left behind as modern fabric production took over. But, like many traditional arts, it is making a serious comeback, and this has placed it firmly back on the 'map of textiles'.

The potential of felt as a textile can be clearly illustrated in the beautiful and skilful work of Sarah Lawrence.

Textile artist

Sarah Lawrence is a textile artist and freelance tutor who specializes in feltwork. She produces 'handrolled' felt which is then embellished with hand or machine embroidery, bead work and gilding (gold paint). Sarah often incorporates other natural fibres into her feltmaking, such as silk, linen, cotton and **ramie**. She also works with embroidery and paper-making.

Sarah's interest in textiles started early, and initially she trained as a teacher of arts and crafts. However, after teaching art and textiles for ten years Sarah decided to give up teaching and, as well as bringing up her two children, embark on a creative embroidery course. Since then Sarah has not looked back, establishing herself as a leading light in the world of creative felt.

A need for felt

Sarah's work is decorative rather than **functional**, but each item is always unique, making it a one-off production. She has exhibited her work throughout the UK and Europe, and has been asked to make wall hangings for individuals, businesses, community centres and even a caribbean cruise liner! When asked to create a textile item, Sarah discusses the client's requirements to find out exactly what they want. The client has usually seen examples of Sarah's work and may want something similar. However, the client may have a particular need which they are hoping Sarah will meet. For example, one business asked for something that would give their meeting room a gentle, calm atmosphere, in complete contrast to the busy office outside and the town beyond.

Making felt

Given the scale of Sarah's work, it is a surprise to discover that she produces all her feltwork in her own home. In her own words, this is how she creates a design in felt:

> 'The method of felt-making I use comes from Central Asia. It involves two steps, **pre-felting** and **milling**. I prefer to use Merino 70 wool that has been pre-dyed. First, I create the bottom layer of felt by pulling out 'tiles' or fibres from the fleece and laying them in one direction on a piece of cane blind or bubble wrap (depending on the size of felt). I then create the next layer in the same manner but laying the fibres in the opposite direction. These two layers form the basis of the felt, although

This is a fine example of Sarah Lawrence's colourful feltwork. She often embellishes her felt with embroidery, bead work and gilding.

further layers can be added. It is very important that each layer is the same thickness. Each layer could be a different colour, depending on the effect you wish to create.

'So far the body or structure of the felt has been formed and I think of this as the "canvas" on which I will create a design. However, instead of painting, I place carefully chosen pieces of coloured fleece on to the body of the felt. The decorative fibres may be one or two layers thick. The felt then goes through the pre-felting process.

'My felt is known as pre-felt because it generally has a shrinkage rate of 30%. It is possible to continue **hardening** and milling or shrinking the felt until there is no further movement.'

Inspired ideas

Sarah believes it is crucial to carry a sketchbook! Whenever she comes across anything inspirational which could be used in one of her designs she sketches it, even though she may not use it immediately. Her main influences come from the things she particularly likes, such as Indian or Persian objects, designs from the Victorian era, or flowers and birds. When it comes to the actual felt-making, Sarah feels the design is partly created by the process itself – by the flow and movement of the colours, along with the layering and texturing of the fibres. **Motifs** play an important part in Sarah's designs, although she chooses to use simple shapes like fish, stars, hearts and birds. These motifs provide a constant supply of ideas, because by changing just one element a whole new design can be created. Sarah believes that her creativity comes from limiting herself to certain influences, shapes and designs.

manufacturing fabrics

Companies manufacturing fabric on a large scale use high-speed looms, often with computer systems and electronic sensors. The two most common types of weaving used today are shaft weaving and Jacquard weaving. Shaft weaving produces plain, twill and sateen woven fabrics (see page 7). These weaves are fairly uniform in design because the **warp** and **weft yarns** are held in position by a frame on the loom. Jacquard weaving (see page 9) produces fabrics with more complex designs and patterns.

Industrially produced knitted fabric is also produced by machines, either flat-bed or circular knitting machines. Tubes of fabric are made using circular knitting machines.

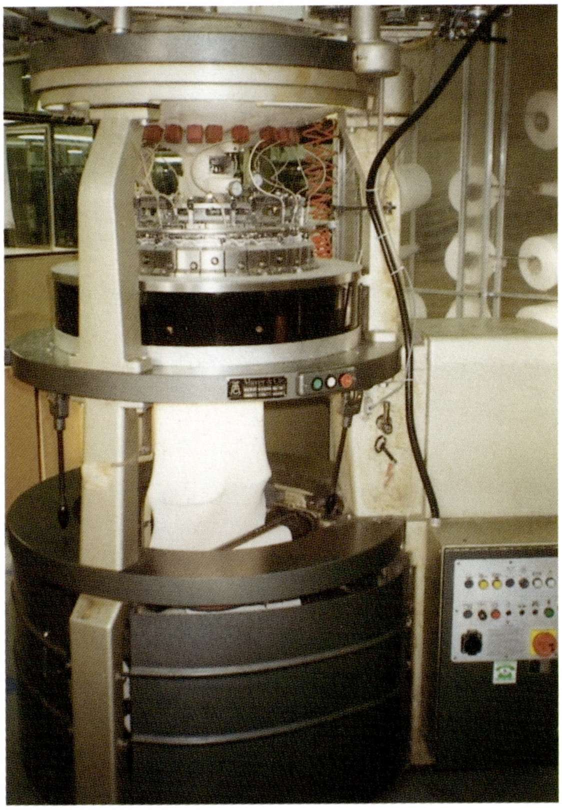

Hunters' mill – a case study

Fabric production is still confined mainly to northern Britain, although traditionally the reason for this was that those areas had easy access to a great deal of wool. Large and small scale fabric production can be found in Lancashire, Yorkshire and Scotland. The following case study is about a Scottish company called Hunters of Brora. They are spinners and manufacturers of woollen fabrics who specialize in tweeds, rugs and woollens. They also provide fabrics for menswear companies like Austin Reed, Burberry and DAKS Simpson.

Hunters of Brora have a long history of designing and making woollen clothes. The business recently moved to a new mill, built specifically to meet their manufacturing requirements.

The company have designed and produced a whole range of Scottish 'checks' over the years, and they have even included less traditional colours, such as bright orange, and yarns such as **bouclé**. Having the ability to keep pace with changing consumer demand, while continuing to produce more traditional fabrics, is important for a fabric manufacturer. The company use materials such as Cheviot wool, Scottish Shetland wool, New Zealand Merino wool and Australian lamb's wool. Each type of wool gives different qualities to the yarn and therefore to the fabrics they produce.

A circular knitting machine produces fabric in a tube. The fabric is used in the production of skirts, dresses, vests and tops.

In addition, Hunters can blend wool with other fibres like silk, mohair, alpaca, angora and manufactured **staple fibres**.

Flowline production

Hunters' new mill has enabled them to use a system of 'flowline production' for the manufacture of their fabrics. This means they develop new products while continuing to produce their traditional cloths in the traditional way. The system is ideal for a business that is based on small fabric **runs** but has a fast **turnaround**.

To spin and manufacture woollen cloth successfully, it is crucial that the methods of blending and **carding** are correct. Hunters use a system of blending that is highly accurate, an important factor when fabrics are produced in anything from pure white to complex but subtle heather mixtures.

The carding machine used by Hunters is also particularly suited to their requirements. They produce short runs of wool, and other raw materials, that are spun into high-quality yarns, so the carding machine needs to have variable speed drives, a data control system and an energy-efficient drive. The data control system allows information about production and efficiency to be viewed on a colour screen, and the energy-efficient drive means energy use is low, saving on production costs. Hunters' new machinery also means that production can be switched quickly from clothes and furnishing yarns to hosiery yarns, giving them more flexibility.

Tasteful colours

In addition to their new production system, Hunters have also recently installed a new dyeing process. Their dyehouse is now able to dye fibres loose or on cones, which enables their designers to create a wider and more varied range of colours. Nature is frequently used as inspiration for their shades, for example 'sunshine', 'peach blossom', 'green heather' and 'evening sky'.

A wider range of colours can now be created with Hunters' new dyeing process.

open-work fabrics

Lace is described as an **open-work fabric** because it has a very loose structure. It consists entirely of fine threads, some of which are twisted around others at intervals. The pattern is formed by the shape of the holes that are created, as well as by their positioning in the fabric. Traditionally, lace was made by hand, a time-consuming and complicated process, but today it can be produced quickly and easily using machines. It is produced in cotton or manufactured fibres and is sold at a range of prices. These vary depending on whether they are sold to retailers or manufacturers.

There are a surprising number of ways to create a lace fabric by hand.

Needlepoint lace

This type of lace is made using a needle, some thread and strips of tape or braid. One particular style of needlepoint lace, known as Renaissance lace, was popular in Victorian times. To produce this lace various buttonhole stitches are worked between sections of tape or braid so the stitches are actually anchored by the tape. The tape or braid becomes part of the lace fabric and must be flexible enough to curve with the lines of the design or pattern.

Filet lace netting

As its name suggests, this type of lace-work produces a fabric that looks like netting and may be strong enough for use as a hammock or delicate enough to become a decorative cloth. Its construction is based on knotting to produce a mesh which is worked in a square or diamond shape, with a design embroidered on it. Like needlepoint lace, it has a long history and was very popular in Europe during the seventeenth century.

Tatting

Tatting is another form of lacework that involves knotting. The knots, known as double stitch, are worked on top of single threads, creating a delicate-looking but strong fabric. The designs for tatting are all based on rings and chains, and only small samples tend to be produced. Rather than a needle, tatting is created using a small shuttle; a **continuous filament** is wound around the shuttle which is then manoeuvred around loops of thread. Tatted lace used to be fashionable along the edge of collars on dresses.

Bobbin lace

Bobbin lace is probably the technique most people associate with lace-making. It dates back to the fifteenth century, and as its popularity spread worldwide, local styles developed and were named according to their place of origin – Chantilly lace, Honiton lace and Nottingham lace are some examples. Today there are still a few places where bobbin lace is made by hand; in India, Sri Lanka, Turkey and Belgium the craft is a popular tourist attraction.

Bobbin lace uses only two basic stitches, but from these a whole array of complex designs can be woven. Threads are wound on to bobbins (small reels) and the lace is worked on a pillow or padded board. A paper pattern is laid out beneath the lace. Pins are inserted through the pattern into the pillow to hold the threads in place, and the bobbins are manipulated by the lace-maker according to the set design. The number of threads or bobbins used can range from a few pairs to several hundred!

Traditionally silk, linen or metallic threads were used to create bobbin lace, and the bobbins were made from wood, bone or ivory. Today, cotton is a more practical choice, and bone and ivory bobbins have largely been replaced with plastic. However, turned wooden bobbins are popular and perhaps have a more aesthetic appeal than the plastic versions. Bobbins are sometimes 'spangled' – weighted down to keep the threads taut; this may be done with glass beads, which adds to their attractiveness.

Lace weaves

Lace can also be created using a weaving technique. However, lace weaving varies from the conventional type because the **warp** and **weft** threads are not always at right angles to one another. Instead, they are sometimes diverted to form spaces in the weave, so creating an open-work fabric.

Lace weaving can be worked on a simple frame loom or on a complex mechanical one, the purpose of which is to keep the warp threads evenly spaced and taut while the weft is passed over and under according to the pattern.

Bobbin lace being produced using weighted or 'spangled' wooden bobbins.

creative carpets

Carpets consist of two parts: fibres on the surface known as the **pile**, and a backing to hold the fibres in place. Some carpets have an additional foam layer called an underlay attached to the backing; but usually the underlay is separate from the carpet, and it is sometimes made of felt. The underlay is needed because it helps to give the carpet 'bounce', prevents dust and dirt from below the floorboards getting into the carpet, and acts as a layer of heat insulation.

Carpet traditions

In the past only wealthy people could afford carpets in their homes. Today, not only are most homes carpeted but offices, shops, some schools and even trains and coaches are too. Carpets are now more cheaply produced, and living standards have risen.

Traditionally, carpets were made by weaving the pile and the backing at the same time. The pile was made from wool while the backing was created using **jute**, a natural plant fibre which is quite stiff and hard-wearing.

Modern carpets

Today many carpets are backed with **polypropylene** rather than jute because it is cheaper to produce and is very tough and hard-wearing. Wool is an ideal fibre for carpet manufacture as it is durable and soft to the touch. However, wool is now often blended with manufactured fibres such as polypropylene or **polyester** because this improves the strength. Carpets that are 100% polypropylene or nylon are available and are less expensive than all-wool carpets; they are also easier to clean, but can cause static electricity.

Making carpets

The two main types of traditional woven carpet are Axminster and Wilton.

Axminster

Axminster carpets are usually colourful and highly patterned because it is easier to generate designs with this type of weave. Many are a blend of 80% wool and 20% nylon, and they normally have a velvet (cut) pile. The process of weaving an Axminster carpet means the pile and the backing are produced at the same time. The tufts created by the pile **yarn** are held in position by **weft** threads which form the backing.

Wilton

Wilton are the most hard-wearing carpets. They are expensive because quality materials like pure wool are used and their designs are complex. They are woven on Jacquard looms (see page 9). The yarns are held over wires running across the carpet, then secured by weft threads which also create the backing. The wires are used to form pile loops, after which they are withdrawn or, if a cut pile is required, the wires cut the loops as they are withdrawn. When a yarn is not required for part of a pattern, it is carried in the backing, adding stability and strength to the carpet.

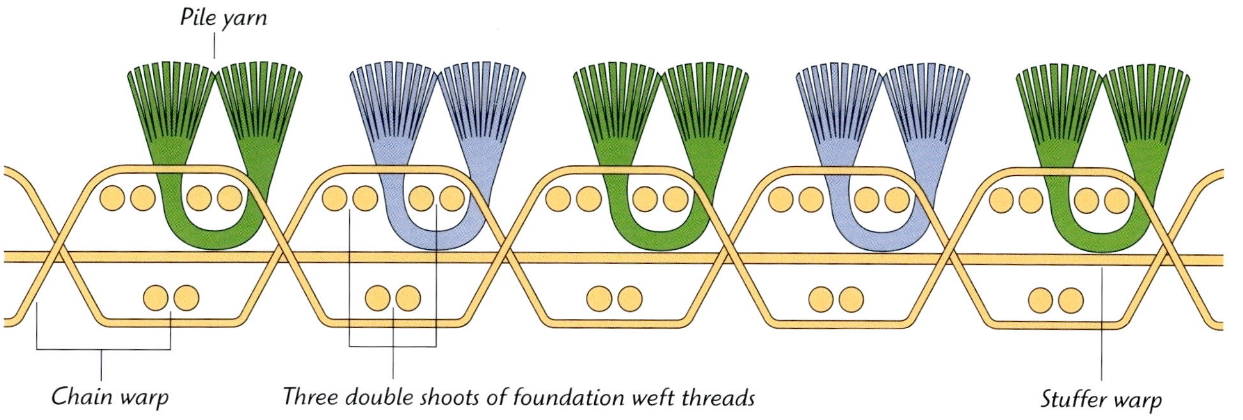

The construction of typical machine-woven Axminster carpet. One of the weft threads secures the pile tufts.

Modern methods

Tufted carpets are less expensive to manufacture and buy, and can be made from virtually any fibre. The process is relatively simple, but it is a high-speed, high-volume, **automated production**. The pile on tufted carpets is attached to a pre-woven backing. It is created by stitching yarn through the backing cloth, creating loops on the surface which may be cut or may remain as loops. The stitched yarn is held in place by a coat of **latex** applied to the reverse, and a secondary backing is then added. These carpets tend to be plain, although patterns can be created through the use of texture, such as with velvet or twist and loop pile.

Flocking is a relatively new method of carpet construction, and again the backing is produced separately. Woven or non-woven fabrics are coated with adhesive, and the fibres are then dropped loosely on to the surface. Sometimes they lie flat and sometimes they stand upright because of a static charge on the backing which attracts one end of the fibre. These carpets are good at resisting dirt, dust and liquids, so they are popular floorings for kitchens.

Natural flooring

The Original Seagrass Company Ltd started in the 1980s in order to meet a growing consumer demand for natural floor coverings. They use natural fibres and natural weaving techniques to produce durable but attractive floorings. The fibres they use are restricted to those the company knows will work best in the home: seagrass, coir, sisal and wool.

Seagrass is grown mostly in China, as it needs a paddy field environment and a hot climate. It is a hard, almost **impermeable** fibre which is spun into tough strands that are naturally stain-resistant. Coir is the outside matting of a coconut shell and is imported mainly from India. It is a tough, rugged fibre used for matting and flooring. Sisal comes from the leaves of the tropical agave plant. It is a rope-like fibre that can be woven to produce intricate patterns. Jute is sometimes used in a blend with other fibres, for example sisal/jute, as it is not strong enough to be used alone.

functional fabrics

▲ *Sports fabrics should have good wickability. This person snowshoeing should feel comfortable despite working hard in a cold climate.*

All fabrics have a function in terms of meeting the needs of a particular textile item. Clothes must not be see-through (unless you particularly want them to be!), carpets must feel soft, bandages must protect a wound... However, the term '**functional** fabrics' refers to fabrics that are used for a very specific purpose, such as:

- sportswear for diving, rock climbing, sailing, hiking, running etc.
- workwear such as **flame-retardant** overalls
- clothes worn in arctic conditions.

Sportswear

Many sports activities place great demands on sportswear and the fabrics used. One requirement of a whole variety of sportswear is that of moisture absorption. To put it crudely, anyone who carries out strenuous exercise will sweat as they do it! The aim of this type of functional fabric is to allow the sportperson to sweat with as little discomfort as possible.

In everyday circumstances, when the temperature and humidity (the amount of moisture in the air) are normal for that location, and when a person's activity level is normal, the body perspires in order to regulate its own temperature. This perspiration evaporates within the layers of the skin and is released in the form of water vapour, which is invisible.

Cold and clammy

Liquid sweat usually appears only when the temperature and humidity of the air are very high or the person is taking strenuous exercise. The moisture that forms on the skin, and sometimes on the clothing, requires a means of escape, or else the skin feels cold and clammy, making the person uncomfortable and probably unable to concentrate properly.

Water vapour and air have different methods of passing through fabrics. All textile fibres are **impermeable** to air, which means that it cannot pass through the fibres, only the spaces in between. Water vapour, however, can pass through fabric in the same way as air and, sometimes, it can also travel through the fibres, evaporating at the same time. Water vapour can pass through all absorbant fibres such as cotton, viscose and wool.

Wickability

Wickability describes the way moisture runs along a fibre even if the fibre is completely non-absorbant. The term is borrowed from the idea of a candle wick, which, once lit, takes wax from its surroundings in order to keep the flame alight. In the context of a fabric, once the moisture has travelled along the fibre it then evaporates on the outside of the fabric, keeping the skin dry and cool. If the fibres do not absorb moisture, the fabric will actually dry more quickly.

Sporting layers

This is where textile technology steps in. Recent developments have produced sportswear fabrics that have layers made of various fibres. The inner layer is non-absorbant and has good wickability, whereas the outer layer is a highly absorbant fibre. The theory behind this is that perspiration on the skin will quickly travel along the fibres of the inner fabric, then the outer fabric will absorb the moisture, which gradually evaporates. Usually a manufactured fibre is chosen for the inner fabric and a natural fibre, like cotton, for the outer fabric.

Breathability

It has already been mentioned that air has to pass through the spaces beween fibres in order for the fabric to 'breathe'. The traditional method for producing breathable fabrics was to create them with an open weave, allowing space for air to circulate.

The first breathable fabric was manufactured back in 1888. It was a woven **cellular fabric** called Aertex, a name which many people still associate with the functional sports top for which the fabric became famous. Recently there has been an Aertex revival and the fabric has been revamped to make it more modern and fashionable. The cellular structure remains, along with its breathable qualities, but it now has a more textured and modern feel.

Aertex fabric as it looks today. The fabric has an open weave that allows air to circulate and keep you cool.

working clothes – a case study

Back in the 1970s a Swedish electrician named Matti Viio identified a need for **functional** and comfortable working clothes. He knew how impractical the conventional 'bib and braces' were for electricians: braces slid off shoulders, buttons came loose and waistbands gaped, leaving little to the imagination.

Consequently, Matti decided to make his own clothes for work, ones that were practical as well as fashionable. Although an electrician wearing flares to work (it was the 1970s) caused a bit of a stir, it was also the beginning of Snickers® Original.

Snickers® Original

Matti Viio had the idea that 'professional craftsmen and women should have working clothes that are on a par with their finest tools and their own professional expertise'. He believed that comfort at work and efficiency were inseparable, so he designed and made clothes specifically for the workplace. Gradually the interest in dressing functionally and smartly at work became popular with workers and their bosses. By 1981 Snickers® were ranked as one of Sweden's 100 most important **innovations**.

Snickers® today

The type of workwear currently being produced by Snickers® Original Ltd is a far cry from the flared trousers Matti first designed. Snickers® now manufacture 'product systems' with a high degree of flexibility to suit all workers. Snickers® believe that the service and maintenance sectors are the industries of the future, and have developed product systems to serve the ever flexible professional person.

Snickers® FlexiPocket™

According to Snickers:

> 'FlexiPocket™ is a system of fixed and movable pockets. It comprises a yoke and an **ergonomically-shaped** tool-

Snickers FlexiPocket™ system. Movable pockets and pouches ensure that the system is as versatile as possible.

belt, which can be worn together or separately. The yoke is very light, strong and comfortable. It has four fixed but hanging pockets, with special compartments and holders for pens, chisels, knives, pliers etc. The pockets are designed to stop tools sliding out.

'All the pouches and pockets in the FlexiPocket™ system are manufactured in hard-wearing, water-repellent and shape-retentive Cordura®.'

Snickers® FlexiLeg™
Kneepads have been around for a long time, but they do not always meet the needs of the worker because they can be cumbersome and uncomfortable. Snickers identified this problem and their solution was the FlexiLeg™, which is an over-trouser fitted with kneepads. Both the kneepads and trousers have a longer life with this flexible system, and as the kneepads are lightweight they are more comfortable to wear. FlexiLeg™ is also available in bright colours with reflective patches.

Snickers® fabric

Snickers® say:

'By continually testing and studying new materials we learn something new every day. The products we launch on the market must, first and foremost, provide the right function and quality at the right price. That is why we are meticulous in our tests, trials and calculations before a new material takes its place in the Snickers® range.'

The current Snickers® range includes: cotton, cotton/nylon, cotton/**polyester**, Pyrovatex-impregnated cotton and Cordura®. Pyrovatex-impregnated cotton is 100% cotton with a special finish added to the fabric that makes it **flame-retardant**. Cordura® is an Aertex-woven fabric made from 100% nylon. It is soft and light as well as resistant to dirt. As it is very strong and hard-wearing it tends to be used for pouches and tool holsters.

Snickers® garments are based on three layers of clothing: an inner, an intermediate and an outer layer. The inner, thermal base layer has special ribbed **terry** cloth on the inside. The intermediate layer can be made of any fabric, but is necessary so that large amounts of air can be trapped between the layers of clothing. The outer layer depends on the nature of the work, but includes windproof and waterproof materials.

Snickers® basic principles

- 'An ingenious system of workwear which can be combined for different tasks and tool requirements. Ideal for indoors, outdoors and in all weather conditions.'
- 'The best possible fit, excellent design and a high level of comfort.'
- 'Long life and the potential for combining different garments mean that you don't have to buy new clothes as often. They spare the environment and pay for themselves in the long run.'

protective fabrics

People do not need clothes just to protect them against wet and cold weather. As interest grows in activities such as climbing and sailing, much more specialized clothing is needed. One company that saw the potential of waterproof, breathable fabric was W L Gore & Associates.

Gore-Tex®

More than twenty years ago W L Gore & Associates developed a fabric called Gore-Tex®. It was the world's first reliable and durable waterproof, breathable fabric technology. Gore-Tex® is made by **laminating** a waterproof **membrane** on to a variety of fabrics suited to outdoor conditions.

The result is a fabric that keeps out rain and damp but allows perspiration to pass through. Today Gore-Tex® has a wide range of applications, for example, PacLite®, Activent® fabric, WindStopper®, and Gore-Tex® footwear.

PacLite®

Climbing, backpacking and generally walking the hills have become popular activities. However, although Britain can be relied upon for its beautiful views, it cannot be relied upon to supply equally idyllic weather. The more adventurous, who travel further afield or climb higher up mountains, need protection from low temperatures, rain, hail, snow, wind and generally extreme conditions.

To this end, W L Gore & Associates have created a fabric that is light and comfortable to wear, but which also keeps out the wet. It is used in the manufacture of waterproof, windproof and breathable clothing for mountaineers and backpackers.

PacLite® consists of two layers of Gore-Tex® laminate. The inside layer of the fabric has a **polymer** membrane, with a special patterned structure to protect it. This structure means that PacLite® fabrics do not require a liner, which would add weight to the garment.

How PacLite® works. The weaver is protected from the elements by two layers of fabric. The inner layer has a membrane containing protective dots.

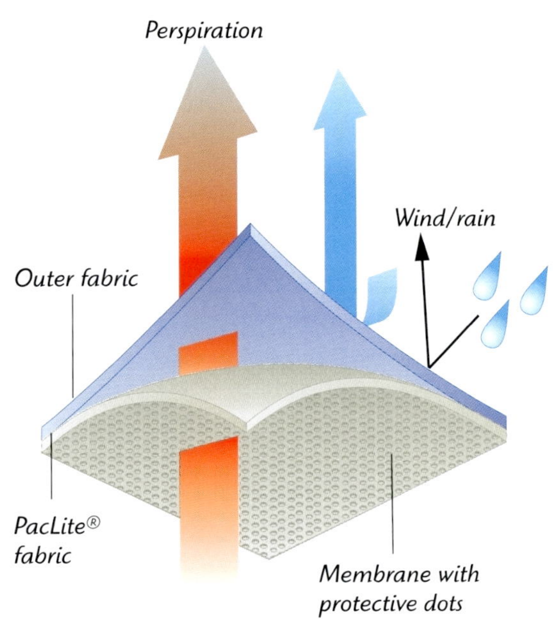

PTFE membrane

The membrane used by Gore-Tex® is manufactured from poly-tetra-fluoro-ethylene (PTFE). It contains millions of tiny holes known as pores. These pores are smaller than water **molecules**, which is how the fabric can prevent rain creeping through to the skin. The pores are large enough for water vapour to pass through so that perspiration can disappear away from the body, through the clothing, and evaporate on the outside. The overall effect is to keep the wearer protected from the elements while remaining comfortable even during intense activity.

Activent® fabric

Activent® fabric provides breathability and water resistance and is windproof in cold, windy conditions, and even during light falls of snow. The technology behind Activent® fabric involves the use of **microporous** films and unique polymers. The barrier it creates forms an ultra-thin and lightweight fabric. Activent® 'breathes' in the same way as Gore-Tex® membranes, but the polymer membrane is different.

The principle of Activent® fabric. The outer fabric is treated with a water-repellent finish; the Activent® fabric on the inside is extremely breathable, water resistant and windproof.

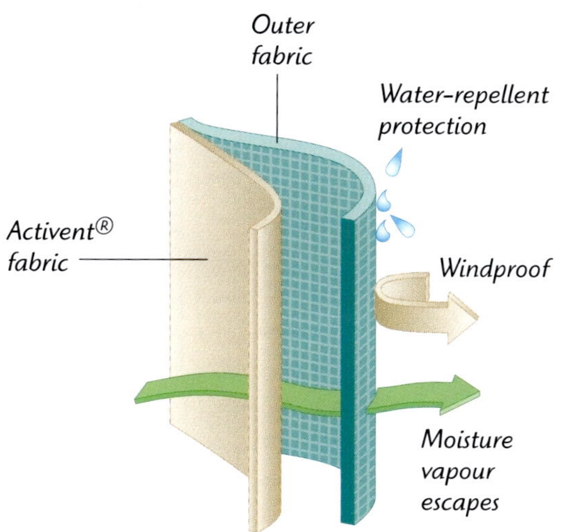

Be seen, be safe

Anybody involved in activities such as mountaineering, climbing or even hill walking, knows the importance of being seen, particularly when daylight fades. For this reason you can now buy some performance clothes, such as jackets, with reflective strips on the shoulder and/or hood. The strips reflect light from torches and means anyone lost on a mountain or in snow can be found more easily.

Permatex®

Permatex® is another example of a breathable, weatherproof fabric. It is used to make linings and outer fabrics for activity clothing and footwear, as well as sportswear, workwear and some fashion garments. Permatex® is a lightweight, hydrophillic (water-loving) **polyurethane** material, which can be used as a membrane on both natural and **synthetic** fabrics. It works by allowing perspiration to diffuse through the membrane and at the same time stopping water droplets from entering.

What is water resistance?

There is no agreed standard test for water resistance, and the test for waterproofness does not allow for fabrics that are slightly or partly resistant to water. However, a water-resistant fabric should also be water-repellent, which means beads of water will form on the fabric's outer surface. Activant® fabric, for example, is water-resistant but not waterproof.

fashionable fleece

A fleece fabric is a knitted fabric with a fleecy **pile** surface. The production of fleece fabrics was originally based on that of tufted carpets, although the fabrics were easier to make because both the material and machinery were lighter. Fleece fabric has been used in the manufacture of jackets ('fleeces') for cold conditions for many years now. However, technological developments have meant that, as a fabric, fleece has become highly effective at insulating the body. In addition, fleece jackets, like many sports clothes, have become popular items of everyday clothing.

Windstopping stuff

Fabrics that have the ability to trap air through their fibre content and construction can provide a layer of insulation for the body. However, this is unlikely to be sufficient when sailing the seas or climbing a mountain. WindStopper® fleece, manufactured by Gore-Tex®, is an example of a high-performance fabric used for garments worn during adventurous activity. There are three categories of WindStopper® fabric:

- windproof liners for sweaters, trousers and casual wear
- windproof fleece for outerwear, gloves, hats and other accessories
- windproof shirts for aerobic sports and casual wear.

What is windproofness?

The term 'windproofness' refers to a fabric's ability to stop wind penetrating through and heat being lost from the body. It is assessed in a rather complicated way that involves measuring the amount of air passing through the fabric – its **permeability** – and measuring the amount of heat lost. Heat loss is tested at different wind speeds because different degrees of windproofness are required for different weather conditions and activities. The Frazier test is an example of a permeability test. Some fabrics are called wind-resistant rather than windproof, and so they are a less effective form of protection.

WindStopper® fabric

The diagram below shows how the WindStopper® **membrane** is constructed. WindStopper® fabric is produced by **laminating** the membrane on to the particular high-performance fabric. This membrane (known as ePTFE) is extremely lightweight and durable, and despite stopping the wind, still allows breathability.

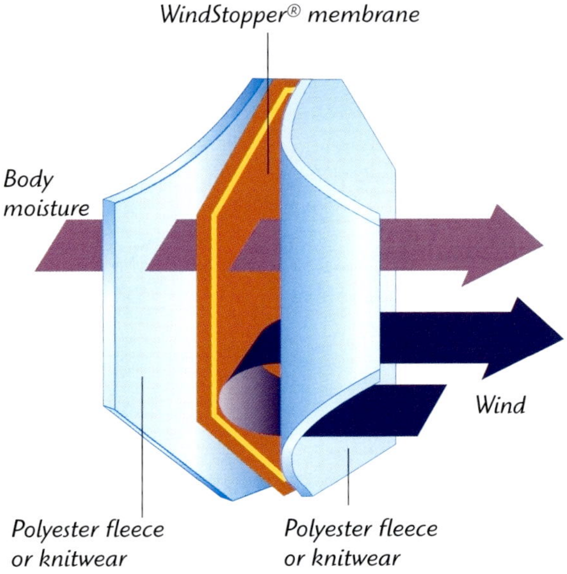

*The extremely light and elastic WindStopper® membrane is placed between two **functional** layers of textile.*

Environmentally friendly fleece

Unlikely though it may sound, fleece fabric can now be made by recycling plastic bottles! This environmentally friendly fleece is produced by breaking recycled plastic into chips which are then **extruded** into a fibre. The fibres are spun to form a **polyester** yarn and knitted into fleece fabric. This new fleece is known as Malden's Polartec Recycled Fabric and has the advantage of being kind to the environment by reducing waste and pollution.

Fleece tops, like many sports clothes, have become popular items of everyday clothing.

Ventilation

Breathable fabrics play an important role in ventilation of the skin. Ventilation is the free circulation of air within an area, in this case surrounding the body. During everyday activity, lack of ventilation is not usually a problem; but when a person's activity level increases, the energy they expend creates heat and moisture (perspiration) and so the need for efficient ventilation arises. Breathable fabrics have played a major part in making activity clothes more comfortable, as they allow moisture to move away from the body and air to circulate around the skin.

The amount of ventilation a body gets depends on a number of factors:

- type of fabric worn. A garment made from a tightly woven **polyamide** fibre with a waterproof finish is likely to cause a problem with ventilation. The fibre and **yarn**, construction and finish all contribute to air circulation.
- shape of garment worn. Tight-fitting clothes obviously restrict the amount of air passing to and from the body.
- kind of outfit worn. Layers of clothing create pockets of air between each layer.
- external conditions, such as the amount of activity and the climate.

Brushed fleece

Fabric can be given a finish known as brushing, which literally brushes the fabric's surface. The fabric passes over rollers covered with wires that lift the fibre **ends** and raise the pile. A fabric treated in this way can trap more air and so provide more insulation than it would normally. An example of a fleece fabric treated in this way is Trevira® fleece, used in the manufacture of outdoor and activity wear.

stretch fabrics

A relatively recent development in **synthetic** fibres has been the production of microfibres. These are extremely fine fibres with characteristics that match some natural ones, but the fabrics they produce are much easier to care for. Elastane is an example of a microfibre.

Elastane

Elastane is a synthetic fibre with the ability to extend up to five times its original length before it breaks. Fabrics may have small amounts of elastane added to them when stretch properties are required. They can be found in swimwear, lingerie and stretch trousers and tops. Elastane is the **generic name** for this group of fibres, and **brand names** include Lycra® made by DuPont.

Lycra®

The development of Lycra® has greatly influenced the direction of the clothing industry, particularly in the areas of fashion, sport and leisure. Figure-hugging clothes have provided freedom of movement for the young and old alike, whether fashion-conscious or simply looking for comfort and convenience.

Little or lots

A stretchy garment made using Lycra® is likely to show the percentage of added Lycra® on its **care label**. There may be as little as 2%, but this will still have quite an affect on the fabric, allowing it to stretch and drape easily. Fabrics that are designed for really close contact, in garments such as swimwear, may contain as much as 40% Lycra®.

Lycra® is an extremely fine filament – finer than a human hair, so it is difficult to measure its thickness. For this reason a

Fabrics with stretch properties allow figure-hugging clothes to move with your body.

measurement known as decitex is used, which actually refers to the weight of the **yarn**. 10,000 metres are weighed in grams, and yarns can vary from 11 decitex which is the finest to 1880 decitex which is the thickest.

Technicalities

Like all elastane fibres, Lycra® has a complex chemical structure with long flexible sections of **molecules** joined to shorter, more rigid sections. When the fibres are stretched, the folded sections straighten out and the shorter rigid sections remain together. This means a fabric made using these fibres will stretch when a force is applied. Once the force is removed, the molecules within the fibres revert back to their folded position and the fabric returns to its original size.

Adding Lycra®

Lycra® comes in dull white, semi-transparent bright yarns and clear yarns which can be added to both woven and knitted fabrics. To join Lycra® with other yarns during fabric production, the Lycra® is usually given a covering of the other yarns so it disappears completely into the body of the fabric. This process of covering or 'sheathing' the Lycra® has two particular advantages:

- it ensures the main fibres' characteristics (appearance, feel etc.) are retained
- it enables certain weaving and knitting techniques to take place because the Lycra® is made temporarily stable.

Covering Lycra®

There are three main ways to cover Lycra® fibres: single/double covering, core-spinning and interlacing.

- Single/double covering – involves wrapping either one or two strands of yarn around a Lycra® yarn that has been stretched. If two yarns are used then they are wrapped in opposite directions to provide more stability.
- Core-spinning – involves spinning the other yarns around a 'core' yarn of Lycra®. Once again the Lycra® is first stretched and completely surrounded by the non-elastic yarns.
- Interlacing – involves applying jets of air to the other yarns, causing them to interlace with the stretched Lycra® yarn in the centre. The resulting yarn has a loopy surface owing to the random nature of the interlacing, so it is particularly useful for producing knitted fabrics.

All shapes and sizes

The ability of fibres like Lycra® to stretch and recover has provided consumers of all shapes and sizes with a much wider choice of clothes for their wardrobe. For example, the addition of Lycra® to garments like jeans means they are not available just for people whose figure matches the manufacturers' average size. Also, underwear with panels of stretch fabric is available to help the wearer achieve a 'flat stomach'.

textile projects

Being able to recognize fabrics is an important part of textile knowledge. However, because of the expansion in textile technology and science, there are thousands of fabrics available today, and it is often incredibly difficult to identify one from another!

Project 1

If you want to expand your knowledge of fabrics, it may be worth trying to create your own fabric 'dictionary'. This isn't something you're likely to complete immediately; but once you've started it you can continually add to it, and it will help improve your awareness of different fabrics.

1. You will need: a variety of different fabric pieces (off-cuts etc.) that you can identify; scissors; glue stick; 26 sheets of thin card (A4 size); plastic wallets; A4 file.
2. Cut each fabric into a square 3cm x 3cm, or a circle with a 3cm diameter.
3. Use a separate card sheet for each letter of the alphabet (e.g. all fabrics beginning with A will go on the first sheet etc.).
4. Stick each fabric sample on to the appropriate sheet using the glue stick, and label it with the fabric's name.
5. To develop the dictionary further you could add the current cost of the fabric (per metre) and list its main properties.
6. Place the sheets in plastic wallets and store them in a ring-binder.

Your dictionary file should become a useful source of reference whenever you work with textiles.

Project 2

Textile wall hangings, collages and pictures have become very 'vogue' recently. In other words they're trendy items to have in the home or workplace! Create your own wall hanging, collage or picture using a particular fabric or range of fabrics, by following these steps.

1. Consider the fabric(s) you'll use – felt? lace? woven? knitted? recycled?
2. Think about joining that fabric (or fabrics). Will you use fabric glue, machine stitching, hand sewing, or a combination of these?
3. On what will you base your design? Will it be polygon shapes, as in patchwork; a theme of recyling; inspiration from music; a hobby or interest?
4. Who will the wall hanging be for and where will they hang it? This may affect the design and colour scheme you choose.
5. Produce a rough sketch of your design.
6. Develop the design, adding detail and colour.
7. Plan the size of the work and how you'll hang it. An effective and simple way of framing is to use bamboo cane (available at most garden centres and DIY stores) through the top and bottom of the backing fabric.

Fabric properties

The chart opposite gives an indication of the properties of certain fabrics. You must remember that these will depend on the fibres from which they are made, the method of construction, and any processes that have been applied to them.

Fabric	Popular uses	Main properties
Cotton (fabrics made using cotton – calico, cambric, chintz, cordroy, damask, denim, drill, flannelette, gaberdine, Oxford, poplin, terry towelling)	towels, tea towels, underwear, shirts, baby clothes, dresses, tops, duvet covers, jeans, jackets, sheets, trousers	• water-absorbant • fairly strong • cool to wear • soft to the touch • good conductor of heat
Wool (fabrics made using wool – delaine, felt, flannel, gaberdine, melton, serge, tweed, velour)	jumpers, blankets, carpets, bags, suits, dresses, coats, hats, underfelt, rugs	• water-absorbant but felts easily • warm to wear • good insulator • good elasticity • crease-resistant • drapes well
Silk (fabrics made using silk – chiffon, crêpe, crêpe de Chine, damask, dupion, duchesse, georgette, organza, satin, shantung, taffeta)	cushions, wall hangings, shirts, underwear, bedclothes, shirts, scarves, wedding/evening dresses, ties	• excellent drape • soft to the touch • cool to wear • reasonable elasticity • water-absorbant • strong
Linen (fabrics made using linen – cambric, brown holland, damask, lawn)	shirts, skirts, trousers, tops, dresses, curtains, bedding, handkerchiefs, cushions, tea towels, wall hangings	• cool to wear • water-absorbant • strong • poor resilience (creases)
Polyamides (types of polyamide include – nylon, Tactel®)	carpets, jackets, stockings, umbrellas, tents, ropes, bedclothes, ground sheets, ropes, casing for wiring	• excellent strength • very durable • easy-care
Polyester (types of polyester include – crimplene, Dacron®, Terylene®, Trevira®)	car seat covers, rugs, curtains, pleated skirts, suits, duvet/cushion filling, sails, raincoats	• excellent strength • excellent resilience • water-repellant • easy-care
Viscose (types of viscose include – rayon)	linings for jackets and coats, curtains, trousers, upholstery	• good strength • good dye take-up • reasonable absorbancy
Acrylic (types of acrylic include – Courtelle®, Orlon®)	knitwear, simulated furs and fur fabrics, carpets, suits	• fairly easy-care • warm to wear • good strength • good resilience • reasonable elasticity

recycling fabrics

Recycling is not a new idea but perhaps the incentive behind it has changed over the years. Traditionally fabrics have been 'recycled' mainly for financial reasons, such as passing down clothes through the family so they get maximum wear. Even when clothes did wear out, that was not necessarily the end of their life. Old clothes and other items were cut up to make something new like a patchwork quilt or a rag rug.

Patchwork

Patchwork is the traditional craft of sewing together shapes to form a patterned fabric and is used to produce quilts, cushions and clothes. It is usually formed with polygons (straight-sided geometric shapes) such as hexagons or squares, because they have to fit together without any gaps. Patchwork is a **labour-intensive** job when it is carried out by hand, as every piece of fabric must be carefully joined to the next. Often the stitches are invisible on the right side.

Patchwork patterns

Eventually patchwork became more of a craft than a necessity. Instead of random patterns, intricate designs were being produced. These designs often told stories about families and so started to be passed down the generations.

Modern patchwork

Since World War II, Britain has gradually become a much more affluent society and there has been less need to recycle fabric by making patchwork. Like many aspects of our society, patchwork has taken a move 'up market'– so rather than cut out patches from old clothes and pieces of fabric, ready-cut shapes may be purchased for the production of patchwork items. People today have many more demands placed on them,

Patchwork involves sewing together shapes to form a patterned fabric.

so they do not necessarily have the time to sit and sew anymore.

Machine patchwork

Although still relatively labour-intensive, patchwork can be produced a lot more quickly when it is sewn by machine. With the current interest in environmental issues such as recycling, patchwork has once again become popular. Now, however, it is used more in fashion items such as jeans and jackets than for quilts or cushions.

Rag rugs

Rugs made by plaiting or knotting strips of fabric are another example of a traditional craft item that has become trendy. Like patchwork, part of their appeal today is their 'environmentally friendly' image, and rag rugs can be used as conventional rugs. More expensive versions, however, are made by textile designers and used as wall hangings in the home or workplace.

Natural catwalk

The fashion industry is a big, expensive business with single items of designer clothing being sold for huge amounts of money. However, environmental issues have managed to touch these designers of fashion. During the 1980s, when green issues were becoming very public, top designer Katherine Hamnett started to take on board the consumers' demand to conserve the environment. She began to use unbleached fabrics and chose natural colour schemes for her collections. She also opted for natural fibres like cotton and silk, rather than the manufactured types.

Friendly fibres

The cellulose found in plants and trees is used in the production of cotton and many **regenerated** fibres. However, a recent development has led to the production of a more ecologically sound fibre – one that is **biodegradable** and **non-toxic**. Tencel® is the **brand name** for a fibre made using wood pulp from trees grown in **managed forests**. Tencel® is regarded as an environmentally friendly fibre because the trees are continually being replaced, and the manufacturing process does not cause any toxic chemical products to be released into the atmosphere.

Recycled fashion

Fashion is a reflection of the attitudes and experiences of a particular society. So, if the economy is booming, fashions tend to be extravagant and decadent. After World War II, fashions became flamboyant and colourful to show that society had overcome a very serious and difficult time. Contemporary fashions have their own way of reflecting our society's need to be 'seen to be green'. At one time, secondhand shops were thought to be for the very poor and people felt uncomfortable using them. Today, however, their image is very different as they are seen to be helping others, especially those in developing countries. It has become trendy and acceptable to wear secondhand clothes.

versatile textile

The world of textiles stretches far beyond clothes and household items. Textile technology and science have progressed to such an extent in recent years that uses for textile items can be found in the most unexpected places. You can see examples in industry, transport, agriculture, leisure and medicine.

Industrial use

Some more obvious uses of textile items in industry include specialized clothing to protect against chemicals, heat or machinery, or soft furnishings used in aircraft. However, less apparent examples are seen in the building industry where textiles are used in tarpaulin and roofing felt. In civil engineering, railway tracks, roads and reinforcement for embankments all rely on an input from textiles. Industries that use ropes, filters, nets or insulating and strengthening materials – such as the fabric used to reinforce the rubber in car tyres – also depend on textiles.

Use in transport

Once again, there are some obvious uses for textiles here, such as coverings for seats in cars, coaches and trains, as well as seat belts and air bags. Many modes of transport today have some form of carpeting, and air and oil filters are made using textiles. However, if we broaden the term 'transport' even further we can include hot-air balloons, parachutes and even hang-gliders!

Use in agriculture

Anyone who has been involved in growing fruit and vegetables can probably recall using some textile items, such as twine for tying up plants or netting to keep birds away from fruit and berries. Today the use of textiles can be much more technical. For example, mineral fibres can be used as a medium for growing some vegetable crops in greenhouses, while in farming matting can be used for indoor cattle as it is more hygienic than straw.

Leisure-time use

Leisure-time includes holidays as well as sports and hobbies, so the demand for appropriate textiles is enormous. The clothes taken on holiday today are much more **functional** and suited to leisure activities than they were just a decade ago. They are easier to care for while away, they take up less room and are lighter to carry. Which leads us on to luggage ... suitcases and bags are also lightweight and less bulky for convenience when travelling.

Sports, hobbies and leisure activities often require specific clothing, but textiles play an important role in the provision of equipment too. What about artificial ski slopes? Or **synthetic** turf? Musical instruments need protective cases, and of course strings! And where would children (and adults!) be without their ball-pools and bouncy castles?

Medicinal purposes

Textiles have had an enormous impact in the area of medicine in recent years. Dressings, for example, are usually applied to open wounds or burn injuries in order to keep them protected. When the dressing is removed, the last thing the patient wants is for pieces of fabric to

Move into food

Carrington Career & Workwear Ltd supply items of workwear and corporate-wear fabrics throughout Europe. They are also manufacturers of a range of technical performance fabrics for industry.

Carrington produce fabrics for use in garments for areas known as 'cleanrooms'. These are areas where dirt, germs and contamination must be avoided, so the workers are required to wear specialist clothing. Carrington's cleanroom garments have properties such as anti-static and non-linting, and have been used in the electronics and pharmaceutical industries for some time.

Now the technology has been adapted to produce new fabrics for the food industry. The fabrics are known as Astacon 150 and Astacon 180, and they are made from low-linting, fine denier, texturized **polyester yarns**. Obviously it is important that these fabrics act as a barrier between the worker and the food, but they are also constructed in such a way that they let air and water through so the wearer has maximum comfort. They are also very hard-wearing yet easy-care fabrics.

stick to the wound. Special non-linting fabrics that do not shed fibres or fluff have been created for this very reason. Other textiles used in medicine include dissolvable stitches, surgical gowns and gloves, and components of artificial joints.

Most amazing of all, textiles are now being developed with live cells that are compatible with human tissue. In terms of implants, this means that when the item is applied to the body it is less likely to be rejected or cause a reaction.

Textiles make virtually every activity possible – even bouncy castles for children to enjoy!

fabric technology

When **synthetic** fabrics were first produced they were regarded as a cheap alternative to natural ones. Viscose, for example, was originally called 'artificial silk'. However, synthetic fabrics were very much welcomed for their easy-care properties and cheaper prices. Today, although natural fibres are very much back in vogue, consumers are becoming aware of the merits of new fabrics made from microfibres; not as alternatives to natural ones, but in addition to them.

Fashion fabrics

Fashion designers are also recognizing the huge possibilities for these new fabrics. Many have started to work closely with textile designers to ensure their choice of fabric will be completely compatible with their clothing designs. The new fabrics being used include transparent stretch latex, which gives the wearer a 'second skin', or materials that were originally thought of as purely **functional**, such as the non-woven mesh material used in industry. Japanese textile artists such as Jun'ichi Arai have been particularly imaginative in their use of advanced fabrics, combining them with Japanese crafts that are hundreds of years old.

Industrial influence

Developments in industry have greatly influenced the advances that have occurred in textiles. Industry is having to work faster and more cost-effectively than ever. Consequently the materials it uses must be extremely strong but lightweight, and they must be competitively priced as well as serving as many functions as possible. Increasingly in industry, textiles are replacing heavier materials such as metal. The United Kingdom, along with Germany, Belgium, the Netherlands and France, is at the forefront of this new textile technology.

Composite textiles

One area of textile development has been composite fabrics. These are fabrics that are a combination of two or more materials all with different structures. This means the composite fabric has the characteristics of all the materials it contains, which improves its overall performance. Kevlar® is an example of a composite fabric that has been developed by DuPont. It is used when strength is essential, so it is particularly useful for protective clothing.

Geosynthetics

Textile fabrics that are **permeable** to fluids are known as geosynthetics, a term which tends to refer to industrial meshes, nets and mats. They were first used in the 1950s, and today their function is mainly that of reinforcement, for example in filters and drainage.

3D textiles

As most manufactured fabrics are **thermoplastic** they lend themselves to being moulded, and this is now a relatively simple and economic way to produce three-dimensional (3D) fabrics. The fabric is produced as a sheet which is then impregnated with resins. Finally, it is shaped in heated moulds – or the shaping can even take place during the weaving process. Moulded collars, cuffs

Motorcycle gloves made using Kevlar®. The fingers and the back of the hand have been reinforced with Kevlar®, as these areas are the most vulnerable in accidents.

or whole garments have been created by fashion designers, producing rather unusual effects!

Fingerprint fabrics

A rather intriguing development in textiles has been the production of a non-woven, thermally bonded fabric called Colbeck®. It contains fibres with a **polyester** core and a **polyamide** skin which form a random three-dimensional structure. As a result the fabric has a unique pattern that cannot be repeated, and this characteristic has taken Colbeck® from the clothing industry to the world of security and identification cards. The cards look like ordinary credit cards but there is a small transparent hole in them which contains Colbeck® fleece. The structure of the fibre within the fabric is unique, just like a fingerprint, so when the card is read by an infra-red light, the person can be identified as being genuine or an impostor! This concept could have potential for passports and **smartcards** in the future.

Hybrid materials

Hybrid materials have been made partly from textiles and partly from non-textiles, which are hard rather than flexible. Car silencers now use a hybrid material called E-glass roving, which can deaden noise without deteriorating under the heat, vapour and condensation of a car engine. The material also means that silencers can be smaller, allowing more space for the boot, and more scope for designers!

resources

Books

The following books are useful for students studying GCSE Design and Technology: Textiles Technology:

Design & Make It! Textiles Technology Alex McArthur, Carolyn Etchells, Tristram Shepard	Stanley Thornes 1997
Examining Textiles Technology Anne Barnett	Heinemann Educational 1997
Textiles and Technology (UK edition) Adapted by Margaret Beith	Cambridge University Press 1997
Textiles Technology Alison Bartle and Bernie O'Connor	Causeway Press 1997

The following books are useful for more detailed information on fabric production:

The Motivate Series: Textiles Andrea Wynne	Macmillan Education 1997
Textiles Properties and Behaviour in Clothing Use Edward Miller	B T Batsford Ltd 1992

I.C.T.

www.craftscouncil.org.uk/exhib.htm
Provides details of forthcoming arts and crafts events throughout the country

www.sarah-lawrence.com
Provides further information about Sarah's felt-making and exhibitions

www.textile-toolkit.org.uk
Includes news, competitions, details of events and a chat forum for students. There is also a CD-ROM available for use as a teaching aid for GCSE textiles

Places to visit

Quarry Bank Mill, Styal, Cheshire
Built as a cotton spinning and weaving mill in 1784 by Samuel Greg, this is now a working museum of the British Cotton Industry

Victoria and Albert Museum
Cromwell Road
South Kensington
London SW7 2RL
Textile exhibitions and Crafts Council shop

Syon Park, London
(Tel no: 020 8560 0881)
Arts and crafts events and shows throughout the year, an arts centre and needlecraft centre as well as house and gardens to visit

Suppliers of fleece and other craft resources

Wingham Wool Work
Freepost
70 Main Street
Wentworth
Rotherham
South Yorkshire S62 7BR
(Tel no: 01226 742926)

Adelaide Walker
2 Mill Yard Workshops
Otley Mills
Ilkley Road
Otley LS21 3JP
(Tel no: 01943 850812)

Handweavers Studio & Gallery
29 Haroldstone Road
London E17 7AN
(Tel no: 020 8521 2281)

Fibrecrafts
Style Cottage
Lower Eashing
Godalming
Surrey GU7 2QD
(Tel no: 01483 421853)

Hilltop Spinning & Weaving Centre
Hope Farm
Gibbons Brook
Sellindge
Ashford
Kent TN25 6HH
(Tel no: 01303 814442)

International Feltmakers Association
Christine Lewis (Secretary)
Wyndhurst
Piccots End
Herts HP1 3AU
(Tel no: 01442 231159)

Contacts

The Crafts Council
44a Pentonville Road
London NI 9BY
(Tel no: 020 7278 7700)
Provides up-to-date information about arts and crafts exhibitions and shows; also produces a magazine called Crafts, *available on subscription*

glossary

automated production production that uses machinery

bias runs diagonally across the fabric weave and is where the fabric has some stretch

biodegradable able to be broken down (decomposed) by bacteria

bouclé yarn or fabric with thread looped at intervals throughout

brand name the trademark of a fabric or item which cannot be given to anything else

carding a type of combing process which pulls fibres to make them parallel with each other, and then separates them to form a sliver (rope)

care label label sewn into textile items to indicate how they should be laundered and cared for

cellular fabric a loosely woven fabric with spaces to allow air to circulate

colourways the same design shown in different colours

continuous filaments long fibres that are produced naturally or manufactured in one length

ends in weaving, this refers to the warp yarns

ergonomically-shaped designed with working conditions in mind, in order to achieve maximum efficiency

extruded in spinning, this refers to the forcing of a liquid through tiny holes in a spinneret

flame-retardant a finish added to fabrics to prevent them catching light; often it makes them self-extinguishing

functional having a very specific function and specialized end-use, e.g. a thermal fabric (for warmth)

generic name name used to describe a group or class of fibres, fabrics etc.

geotextiles textiles used in industries such as civil engineering

hardening the final part of the felting process when the felt is rolled vigorously

heddle frame used in weaving to lift and lower groups of warp threads

impermeable not allowing something (water or air, for example) to pass through

innovation something totally new and original

jute a natural fibre, rather coarse and rough, made from plants

labour-intensive involving a lot of work and taking a lot of time

laminating applying a layer or layers to create a fabric

latex rubber-like fabric

lubricant a substance like oil or grease that helps to keep things moving as they pass one another

managed forests forests in which trees are continually being replaced

membrane a thin film or outer layer of a fabric

molecule very small unit of a substance

motif a repeated image or theme in an artistic work

microporous containing many minute pores or holes

milling the term used to describe the final stage in the process of felting wool; the wool shrinks and becomes dense through firm rolling

nomadic describes a lifestyle that involves wandering rather than staying in one place, often in order to find grazing pasture for herds

non-toxic not poisonous or harmful

open-work fabric a loose fabric such as lace

permeable allowing something (water or air, for example) to pass through

pH a measure of how acidic or alkaline a solution is

picks in weaving, this term refers to weft yarns

pile the fibres on a fabric's surface

polyamide synthetic fibres and/or fabrics made by a process known as polymerization (the joining of polymers)

polyester synthetic fibre or fabric

polymer a natural or synthetic compound that has large molecules made from repeated units of smaller molecules

polypropylene synthetic fibre or fabric

polyurethane synthetic fibre or fabric

pre-felting the first part in the felt-making process, when the fibres are layered in a criss-cross fashion and manipulated; the fibres start to interlock at this stage

ramie a bast fibre (from the plant stem) grown in a hot, rainy climate. It produces a strong fibre, similar to linen

regenerated formed from a mixture of natural and synthetic sources

run amount of fabric produced

smartcards cards containing electronic information; they can be used as swipe cards for identification purposes

staple fibres relatively short fibres (up to about 25cm), compared with the long fibres of continuous filaments

synthetic produced chemically, not naturally

tacking temporary stitches used to hold fabric in position

terry an absorbant cotton fabric, with raised loops left uncut

thermoplastic becoming soft when heated and hard again once cooled

turnaround speed of the production process

warp in weaving, the yarns that run the length of the fabric

weft in weaving, the yarns that run the width of the fabric

yarn single strand of fibres spun together

index

acrylic 37
Activent® 31
Aertex 27
agricultural use 40
Axminster carpets 24

bias 5
bobbin lace 22-3
bonded fabrics 14-15, 43
bouclé 20
breathable fabrics 27, 30, 31, 32, 33

carding machines 21
carpets 24-5
coir 25
Colbeck® 43
composite fabrics 42
continuous filament yarns 11, 12, 14, 22
cotton 4, 23, 27, 29, 37

decitex 35
dyeing fabrics 21

elastane 34
environmental issues 33, 39

fabric properties 36-7
fashion fabrics 39, 42
felt 16-19, 24
felting 16
fibres 4, 14, 21, 33, 35, 39
filet lace netting 22
flame-retardant fabrics 26, 29
fleece 32-3
flocking 25
functional fabrics 26-33, 40, 42

geosynthetics 42
geotextiles 14
Gore-Tex® 30
grain 5

herringbone 7
hybrid materials 43

identifying fabrics 36
industrial use 40, 41, 42

Jacquard weaving 8, 9, 20, 24
jute 24, 25

Kevlar® 42, 43
knitted fabrics
  assembly 13
  interlock fabrics 11
  plain single jersey 10
  purl fabrics 10
  rib or double jersey fabrics 10
knitting 10-13
  hand knitting 10, 11, 13
  industrial knitting 12-13
  warp knitting 11, 12, 13
  weft knitting 10-11, 12, 13
knitting machines
  circular knitting machines 13, 20
  domestic machines 11
  flat bed machines 12, 20
  Raschel machines 12, 13
  Tricot machines 12
  warp knitting machines 12
  weft knitting machines 12

lace 22-3
lace weaving 23
linen 4, 37
looms 4, 6, 8-9, 20, 23
  air and water jet systems 6, 8
  dobby looms 9
  Jacquard looms 8, 9, 20, 24
  projectile system 8
  rapier systems 8
Lycra® 34, 35

manufacturing fabrics 20-1
medicinal uses 40-1
microfibres 34, 42
milling 16-17, 18, 19

needlepoint lace 22
net and mesh fabrics 12

open-work fabrics 22-3

PacLite® 30
patchwork 38-9
Permatex® 31
permeability 26-7, 30, 31, 32, 42
polyamides 8, 33, 37, 43
polyester 15, 24, 29, 33, 37, 41, 43
polymers 30, 31
polypropylene 24
polyurethane 31
protective fabrics 30-1
PTFE membrane 30-1

rag rugs 39
raised-loop fabrics 12, 29
recycling fabrics 38-9
regenerated fibres 39

sateen weave 7, 20
seagrass 25
selvedges 5
silk 37
sisal 25
Snickers® garments 28-9
sportswear 26, 27
staple fibres 14, 21
stretch fabrics 34-5
synthetic fabrics 31, 34, 42

tatting 22
Tencel 39
terry 29
three-dimensional (3D) fabrics 42-3
transport, uses in 40
twill weave 7, 20

ventilation 33
viscose 37, 42

warp and weft yarns 4, 5, 6, 7, 8, 20, 23
water resistance 31
weaving 4-9
  computerized weaving 7, 9
  industrial weaving 8-9
  lace weaving 23
  patterns 6-7
  ScotWeave system 9
  shaft weaving 20
  see also looms
wickability 27
Wilton carpets 24
windproofness 32
WindStopper® 32
wool 4, 16, 20-1, 24, 37
workwear 28-9, 41

yarns 4-5, 6, 7, 8, 11, 12, 14, 20, 22, 23, 24, 33, 35